SALADS

BRIMAR

Editor Angela Rahaniotis
Graphic Design Zapp
Photography Marc Bruneau
Food Preparation / Stylist Josée Robitaille
Assistant Stylist Marc Maula
Tableware courtesy of Stokes and Hutschenreuter

©1994 Brimar Publishing Inc.
338 Saint Antoine St. East
Montreal, Canada H2Y 1A3
Tel. (514) 954-1441
Fax (514) 954-5086

ISBN 2-89433-148-7
Printed in Canada

SALADS

Summer or winter, salads add a note of garden freshness and an element of easy sophistication to mealtime.

With this collection of recipes, you will find new and intriguing ways to present standard salad ingredients as well as the more exotic offerings from the fresh produce section of your supermarket.

You will discover interesting starters such as Cold Purée of Eggplant Salad, and a superb selection of salad side dishes based on simple, yet unusual ingredients such as beets and citrus fruits. You will also discover some exciting main courses, including Curried Shrimp and Rice Salad, and Fresh Halibut Salad.

We have also included 16 easy recipes for salad dressings and mayonnaises that are sure to become family favorites.

Salads are a wonderful way to express your creativity. So use this cookbook as your guide to a fresh look at salads. And enjoy!

WATERCRESS

BOSTON LETTUCE

MÂCHE (CORN SALAD OR
LAMBS' LETTUCE)

ROMAINE LETTUCE

CHICORY

ENDIVES

RADICCIO

SPINACH

ESCAROLE

RED LEAF LETTUCE

DANDELION LEAVES

Choosing and Preparing Ingredients for Salads

•

It is important that the freshest of ingredients be used in salads. Choose vegetables that are in season and ripe.

•

All greens must be washed in plenty of cold water to remove dirt and sand. Dry thoroughly, using a spin-type salad dryer, if available. Watery greens will prevent the dressing from adhering properly.

•

Some salads require time to marinate, others may be served immediately. Unless indicated, salads are best served at room temperature.

How to Peel and Seed Tomatoes

1 Core tomatoes and make an X-shaped incision on the base.

2 Plunge in boiling water just long enough to loosen skins.

3 Remove from water and let cool. Peel off skins.

4 Cut tomatoes in half horizontally or into quarters, or slices. Squeeze out seeds and juice. Chop tomato flesh and prepare to use.

Apple Cole Slaw
(4 to 6 servings)

1	small head cabbage, cored	1
2	apples, cored	2
1	carrot, pared and grated	1
1/2	small onion, grated	1/2
1/4 cup	mayonnaise	50 mL
1/4 cup	plain yogurt	50 mL
1 tbsp	Dijon mustard	15 mL
	salt and white pepper	
	pinch of sugar	
	oil and vinegar to taste	

1 Cut cabbage in four and slice thinly. Place in large bowl. Peel apples and cut into julienne. Add to bowl.

2 Add remaining ingredients, except oil and vinegar, and mix very well.

3 Correct seasoning. Add oil and vinegar to taste. Mix and marinate 30 minutes before serving.

Spicy Creamy Cole Slaw
(4 to 6 servings)

½ cup	sour cream	125 mL
½ cup	mayonnaise	125 mL
2 tsp	English mustard	10 mL
1 tbsp	cider vinegar	15 mL
1 tbsp	horseradish	15 mL
1	head white cabbage, cored and shredded	1
1	carrot, pared and grated	1
1 tbsp	chopped fresh parsley	15 mL
	salt and freshly ground pepper	
	lemon juice to taste	

1 Place sour cream, mayonnaise, mustard, vinegar, salt, pepper and lemon juice in bowl. Mix together. Stir in horseradish.

2 Place remaining ingredients in large bowl. Add dressing and mix well. Cover with plastic wrap and chill at least 4 hours before serving.

Red Leaf Lettuce Salad with Radishes
(4 servings)

1	head red leaf lettuce	1
1	small head Boston lettuce	1
6	radishes, cleaned and thinly sliced	6
¼ cup	toasted pine nuts	50 mL
2 tbsp	Dijon mustard	30 mL
⅓ cup	heavy cream	75 mL
	salt and pepper	
	cayenne pepper to taste	
	lemon juice to taste	

1 Wash lettuces in plenty of cold water and dry thoroughly. Tear leaves into small pieces and place in large bowl. Add radishes and pine nuts.

2 Place mustard, salt, pepper, cayenne pepper and lemon juice in small bowl. Whisk in cream gradually.

3 Pour dressing over salad, toss and serve.

Rice Salad with Crabmeat
(4 to 6 servings)

2 cups	cooked rice	500 mL
½ lb	cooked crabmeat	225 g
1	red bell pepper, peeled and diced	1
½ cup	chopped pimiento pepper	125 mL
½	celery stalk, diced	½
1 cup	pitted black olives	250 mL
2	hard-boiled eggs	2
2 tbsp	wine vinegar	30 mL
1 tsp	Dijon mustard	5 mL
6 tbsp	olive oil	90 mL
1 tbsp	chopped fresh parsley	15 mL
	salt and pepper	
	lettuce leaves	

1 Place rice, crabmeat, red pepper, pimiento pepper, celery and olives in large bowl. Season well and set aside.

2 Slice hard-boiled eggs in half and remove yolks. Reserve whites for other uses.

3 Place yolks in bowl with vinegar. Mash until smooth, then add mustard. Mix well. Incorporate oil and season well. Add parsley and pour dressing over salad. Toss until thoroughly coated. Serve on lettuce leaves.

Pineapple Rice Salad
(4 to 6 servings)

1 ½ cups	steamed rice	375 mL
1 cup	diced fresh pineapple	250 mL
1 cup	sectioned grapefruit	250 mL
4 tbsp	heavy cream	60 mL
	juice of 1 lemon	
	salt and white pepper	
	pinch of paprika	

1 Mix all ingredients together until well incorporated. Correct seasoning.

2 Serve salad on bed of lettuce and decorate with fresh chervil, if desired.

Waldorf Salad
(4 to 6 servings)

2	large apples, cored, peeled and cut in julienne	2
1	celeriac, peeled and in cut julienne	1
½ cup	light mayonnaise	125 mL
2 tbsp	sour cream	30 mL
1 tbsp	chopped fresh parsley	15 mL
1 tbsp	chopped fresh tarragon	15 mL
	juice of 1 lemon	
	Dijon mustard to taste	
	salt and white pepper	
	cayenne pepper to taste	

1 Place apples and celeriac in large bowl. Pour in cold water to cover and add juice of 1 lemon. Let stand 2 hours.

2 Drain well and squeeze out excess water. Place apples and celeriac in bowl.

3 Mix mayonnaise and sour cream together. Add mustard to taste. Stir into salad until evenly coated. Add fresh herbs and seasonings. Mix well.

4 Serve on bed of lettuce leaves.

Easy Salmon Salad
(4 servings)

1 ¼ lb	fresh salmon, cooked, boned and flaked	600 g
1	celery stalk, diced	1
2	shallots, peeled and chopped	2
3	green onions, chopped	3
1	hard-boiled egg, chopped	1
4 tbsp	mayonnaise	60 mL
	salt and pepper	
	juice of 1 lemon	

1 Place salmon and vegetables in bowl. Add hard-boiled egg, mayonnaise, salt and pepper. Mix well.

2 Add lemon juice and mix again. Correct seasoning and serve on mixed greens. Garnish with slices of cooked mushrooms, if desired.

Cooked Vegetable Salad with Creamy Dressing
(6 servings)

1	large boiled potato, peeled and diced	1
½ lb	green beans, pared, cooked and diced	225 g
½ cup	cooked green peas	125 mL
1 cup	cooked white beans	250 mL
1	bunch fresh asparagus, cooked and diced	1
1	small head cauliflower, cooked	1
½ cup	mayonnaise	125 mL
3 tbsp	sour cream	45 mL
	salt and freshly ground pepper	
	paprika and cayenne pepper to taste	
	juice of 1 lemon	
	lettuce leaves	
	chopped fresh parsley	

1 Place all vegetables, except cauliflower, in large bowl. Season well and incorporate 3/4 of mayonnaise and 2 tbsp (30 mL) of sour cream. Add half of lemon juice, mix well and correct seasoning.

2 Arrange salad on bed of lettuce, shaping cavity in middle.

3 Divide cauliflower into florets and place in bowl. Add remaining mayonnaise, sour cream and lemon juice. Season well and mix together. Add paprika, cayenne pepper and chopped parsley to taste.

4 Mound cauliflower in cavity surrounded by vegetable salad.

Spaghettini Salad with Salmon Caviar
(4 servings)

½ lb	spaghettini	225 g
2 tbsp	chopped fresh chives	30 mL
1	shallot, peeled and chopped	1
1 tbsp	extra virgin olive oil	15 mL
2 tbsp	salmon caviar	30 mL
	salt and freshly ground pepper	

1 Cook pasta in salted, boiling water until al dente. Drain well and transfer to large bowl.

2 Add chives, shallot and olive oil. Toss and season well.

3 Serve salad with salmon caviar.

Fresh Mussel Salad with Balsamic Vinaigrette
(4 servings)

3 tbsp	balsamic vinegar	45 mL
1 tbsp	Dijon mustard	15 mL
1	garlic clove, peeled, crushed and chopped	1
1 tbsp	chopped fresh tarragon	15 mL
¾ cup	olive oil	175 mL
12	shrimp, peeled and deveined	12
12	fresh mussels, steamed and shelled	12
1	salmon steak, cooked and flaked	1
10	green beans, pared and cooked	10
10	yellow beans, pared and cooked	10
1	roasted yellow bell pepper, skinned and thinly sliced	1
12	pitted black olives	12
	salt and pepper	
	lemon juice to taste	
	lettuce leaves	

1 Place vinegar, mustard, garlic and tarragon in small bowl. Season well. Add 9 tbsp (135 mL) of olive oil and whisk together to incorporate. Add lemon juice to taste and set aside.

2 Heat remaining oil in frying pan over medium heat. Add shrimp to hot pan and continue cooking 3 minutes over high heat. Season well. Transfer shrimp to large bowl.

3 Add cooked mussels and salmon to bowl containing shrimp. Cut green and yellow beans into 1-in (2.5-cm) pieces and add to bowl. Toss in roasted bell pepper and olives.

4 Season generously and pour in vinaigrette. Mix well and serve over lettuce leaves.

J ulienne Luncheon Salad

(4 to 6 servings)

1	small head romaine lettuce, washed and dried	1
1	head Boston lettuce, washed and dried	1
3	beets, boiled and peeled	3
1	celery stalk	1
4	green onions	4
2	small tomatoes, cored and cut in wedges	2
1 tbsp	chopped fresh basil	15 mL
1 tbsp	chopped fresh parsley	15 mL
½ cup	Mustard Vinaigrette (see p. 86)	125 mL
	salt and pepper	

1 Shred lettuces and arrange on each plate.

2 Cut beets, celery and green onions into sticks. Place in large bowl, add herbs and season with salt and pepper. Pour in vinaigrette and toss.

3 Spoon vegetables in the middle of lettuce. Arrange tomatoes decoratively on lettuce.

4 Garnish with fresh basil leaves, if desired, and serve immediately.

Salad Niçoise
(4 to 6 servings)

I	head Boston lettuce, washed and dried	I
½ lb	green beans, pared and blanched	225 g
I	green bell pepper, thinly sliced	I
I	yellow bell pepper, thinly sliced	I
2	tomatoes, cored, peeled and cut in narrow wedges	2
I	small red onion, peeled and cut in rings	I
¾ cup	solid white tuna	175 mL
¼ cup	pitted black olives	50 mL
¼ cup	Basic Vinaigrette (see p. 89)	50 mL
5	anchovy fillets, drained and chopped	5
3	hard-boiled eggs, quartered	3
	juice of I lemon	
	salt and freshly ground pepper	

1 Tear lettuce leaves into small pieces and place in large salad bowl. Add some of lemon juice, toss and set aside.

2 Place vegetables, tuna and olives in separate bowl. Season well and pour in vinaigrette. Mix well.

3 Spoon mixture over lettuce in bowl. Decorate with anchovies and hard-boiled eggs. Add lemon juice to taste and serve.

Fresh Halibut Salad
(4 servings)

1	onion, peeled and sliced	1
1	celery stalk, sliced	1
1	carrot, pared and sliced	1
1	bay leaf	1
3	fresh parsley sprigs	3
12	black peppercorns	12
1 cup	dry white wine	250 mL
1 ½ lb	fresh halibut	700 g
	salt and pepper / lemon juice	

1 Place 6 cups (1.5 L) water in roasting pan. Add remaining ingredients, except fish, and bring to boiling point over high heat.

2 Reduce heat to low and add halibut. Cook 8 to 10 minutes or adjust time according to thickness. When done, remove from liquid and let cool.

1	celery stalk, diced	1
2	shallots, peeled and chopped	2
½	cucumber, peeled, seeded and diced	½
1 tbsp	chopped fresh parsley	15 mL
1 tsp	chopped fresh chives	5 mL
3 tbsp	mayonnaise	45 mL
	cooked fresh halibut	
	few drops of Tabasco sauce	
	salt and pepper / lemon juice	

1 Carefully bone and flake halibut. Place in large bowl. Add vegetables, fresh herbs and seasonings. Mix together gently.

2 Add mayonnaise and mix well. Squeeze in lemon juice and mix again. Correct seasoning and add more mayonnaise, if desired.

3 Serve salad on bed of radiccio leaves and garnish with wedges of yellow or red tomato, if desired.

Summer Salad
(4 to 6 servings)

3	boiled potatoes, peeled	3
3	celery stalks	3
3	tomatoes, cored, peeled, seeded and sliced	3
1	small red onion, peeled and sliced in rings	1
2	hard-boiled eggs, sliced	2
	salt and pepper	
	Mustard Vinaigrette (see p. 86)	

1 Slice potatoes and celery into julienne. Place in bowl with tomatoes. Season well with salt and pepper.

2 Pour in vinaigrette to taste and mix well. Marinate 30 minutes before serving.

3 Decorate portions with rings of red onion and slices of hard-boiled egg.

Hot Black Bean and Scallop Salad
(4 servings)

2	garlic cloves, peeled, crushed and chopped	2
3 tbsp	wine vinegar	45 mL
1 tbsp	chopped fresh tarragon	15 mL
4 tbsp	olive oil	60 mL
1 lb	fresh scallops, cleaned	450 g
19 oz	can black beans, drained and rinsed	540 mL
1	head Boston lettuce, washed and dried	1
	salt and pepper	
	cayenne pepper to taste	
	chopped fresh parsley	

1 Mix garlic with vinegar, tarragon and oil. Season generously and pour half of mixture in frying pan. Set remaining vinaigrette aside.

2 Heat frying pan over medium heat. When vinaigrette is hot, add scallops and cook 1 minute on each side or adjust time according to size. Using slotted spoon, remove scallops and set aside in bowl.

3 Heat remaining vinaigrette in frying pan. Add black beans and cayenne pepper to taste; cook 3 minutes over high heat. Add beans to bowl containing scallops.

4 Tear lettuce leaves into small pieces and place in large bowl. Add scallops and black beans, toss and correct seasoning.

5 Sprinkle with chopped parsley and serve.

Hearty Lobster and Vegetable Salad
(6 servings)

1	head romaine lettuce	1
1 lb	cooked lobster meat, chopped	450 g
¾ lb	fresh asparagus, cooked and cut in 1-in (2.5-cm) pieces	350 g
½ lb	fresh mushrooms*, cleaned, cooked and halved	225 g
12	water chestnuts, halved	12
12	cherry tomatoes, cored	12
½ cup	mayonnaise	125 mL
½ cup	Ranch Dressing (see p. 95)	125 mL
3 tbsp	chili sauce	45 mL
1 tsp	Dijon mustard	5 mL
	salt and freshly ground pepper	
	lemon juice to taste	
	Tabasco sauce to taste	

1 Wash lettuce in plenty of cold water. Drain well and dry thoroughly. Tear leaves into small pieces.

2 Place lobster, asparagus, mushrooms, water chestnuts and cherry tomatoes in large bowl. Season well.

3 Add lettuce and toss ingredients.

4 Mix mayonnaise, Ranch Dressing, chili sauce and mustard together. Add lemon juice and Tabasco sauce to taste; mix well.

5 Pour dressing over salad and toss well. Serve.

*Refer to Cooking Mushrooms for Salads (page 83).

Warm Mussel and Potato Salad
(4 servings)

4½ lb	fresh mussels, bearded and scrubbed	2 kg
2	shallots, peeled and chopped	2
½ cup	dry white wine	125 mL
2 cups	diced boiled potatoes, still warm	500 mL
½	celery stalk, diced	½
1 tbsp	chopped fresh parsley	15 mL
2	green onions, chopped	2
½ cup	mayonnaise	125 mL
	salt and freshly ground pepper	
	lemon juice to taste	
	few drops of Tabasco sauce	

1 Place mussels, shallots and wine in large pot. Season with pepper. Cover and bring to boil. Cook mussels over low heat until shells open, about 5 minutes. Stir once during cooking.

2 Remove mussels from pot, discarding any unopened shells. Remove mussels from opened shells and place in large bowl.

3 Add remaining ingredients to bowl and season well. Mix and serve on lettuce leaves with slices of lemon.

Green Salad with Gruyère Cheese
(4 servings)

2	heads romaine lettuce, washed and dried	2
2	Belgian endives, cored, washed and dried	2
2	hard-boiled eggs, sliced	2
2	anchovy fillets, drained and puréed	2
3 tbsp	wine vinegar	45 mL
1	shallot, peeled and chopped	1
9 tbsp	olive oil	135 mL
3	anchovy fillets, drained and chopped	3
1 cup	grated Gruyère cheese	250 mL
	salt and pepper	
	juice of ½ lemon	

1 Tear lettuce and endive leaves into small pieces. Place in large bowl with sliced eggs. Season well.

2 Place puréed anchovy fillets in small bowl. Add vinegar, shallot, salt and pepper. Mix well. Add oil and whisk to incorporate.

3 Pour dressing over salad and toss together. Add lemon juice and toss again. Add chopped anchovies, mix and serve. Sprinkle portions with grated cheese. Garnish with mâche and basil, if desired.

Salad of Endives, Potatoes and Pork
(4 servings)

4	large Belgian endives	4
4	boiled potatoes, peeled and sliced	4
6 tbsp	olive oil	90 mL
1	smoked pork cutlet, sliced	1
1 tbsp	Dijon mustard	15 mL
1	shallot, peeled and chopped	1
2 tbsp	balsamic vinegar	30 mL
1 tbsp	chopped fresh parsley	15 mL
	salt and pepper	
	juice of ¹/₂ lemon	

1 Core endives and separate leaves. Wash well in cold water, drain and dry thoroughly. Place in large bowl with potatoes.

2 Heat a few drops of oil in frying pan over medium heat. When hot, add smoked pork and stir-fry 2 minutes. Add pork to bowl. Season with salt and pepper.

3 In small bowl, place mustard, salt, pepper and shallot. Add vinegar and remaining oil; mix together with whisk. Add parsley and lemon juice; mix again.

4 Pour dressing over salad, toss well and serve.

Avocado Salad with Green Beans and Olives
(4 servings)

3 tbsp	lime juice	45 mL
4 tbsp	olive oil	60 mL
3	blanched garlic cloves, puréed	3
I tsp	celery seeds	5 mL
I	large avocado, peeled, pitted and sliced	I
I	small cucumber, peeled, seeded and cut into julienne	I
I	green bell pepper, in julienne	I
I	red bell pepper, in julienne	I
½ lb	green beans, pared, cooked and halved	225 g
½ cup	pitted black olives	125 mL
	pinch of cumin	
	pinch of sugar	
	salt and pepper	

1 Mix lime juice with oil, garlic and celery seeds. Add pinch of cumin and sugar; season well. Whisk to incorporate.

2 Place remaining ingredients in large bowl. Season well. Pour in dressing, toss together and serve.

3 Sprinkle with chopped fresh parsley, if desired.

Romaine Salad with Broiled Chicken
(4 servings)

2	heads romaine lettuce, washed and dried	2
I cup	croûtons	250 mL
I tbsp	soy sauce	15 mL
I tbsp	olive oil	15 mL
2	blanched garlic cloves, puréed	2
I	whole boneless chicken breast	I
½ cup	Ranch Dressing (see p. 95)	125 mL
½ cup	grated Parmesan cheese	125 mL
	salt and pepper	

1 Tear lettuce leaves into small pieces and place in large bowl. Add croûtons, season well and set aside.

2 Mix soy sauce with oil and garlic. Skin chicken and split into halves. Brush mixture over chicken and season well with pepper.

3 Cook chicken in preheated oven set at broil 10 minutes or adjust time according to size. Turn breasts over once during cooking.

4 Add Ranch Dressing to greens and mix well. Divide among dinner plates.

5 Slice cooked chicken on the bias and arrange on lettuce. Sprinkle with cheese and serve at once.

Tossed Greens with Grated Carrot

(4 to 6 servings)

1	head chicory	1
1	bunch watercress	1
3	Belgian endives, cored	3
½ cup	Ranch Dressing (see p. 95)	125 mL
1½ cups	garlic croûtons	375 mL
2 tbsp	grated Parmesan cheese	30 mL
1	large carrot, pared and grated	1
1	apple, cored, peeled and cut in julienne	1
	salt and pepper	

1 Wash chicory, watercress and endives separately in cold water. Drain well and dry thoroughly. Tear chicory leaves into small pieces and place in large bowl with watercress.

2 Pour in dressing and toss until evenly coated. Season with salt and pepper. Toss again.

3 Add croûtons and cheese, mix and divide among plates. Arrange carrot, apple and endive decoratively on greens. Serve.

Cauliflower and Grated Carrot Salad
(4 to 6 servings)

1	cauliflower, blanched	1
2	carrots, pared and grated	2
¾ cup	mayonnaise	175 mL
2 tbsp	sour cream	30 mL
1 tsp	Dijon mustard	5 mL
1 tbsp	chopped fresh parsley	15 mL
	salt and pepper	
	pinch of paprika	
	lemon juice to taste	

1 Divide cauliflower into florets and place in large bowl. Add carrots, season and mix.

2 In small bowl, mix mayonnaise with sour cream and mustard. Add dressing to salad and mix well.

3 Season with salt, pepper and paprika. Add lemon juice to taste. Sprinkle with parsley and serve.

Stuffed Tomato Salad
(4 servings)

4	large tomatoes	4
½ lb	fresh shrimp, cooked, peeled, deveined and finely chopped	225 g
1	shallot, peeled and finely chopped	1
1 tbsp	chopped fresh parsley	15 mL
1	celery stalk from celery heart, finely chopped	1
3 tbsp	mayonnaise	45 mL
1 tsp	Dijon mustard	5 mL
1	bunch watercress, washed and dried	1
¼ cup	Mustard Vinaigrette (see p. 86)	50 mL
	salt and pepper	
	lemon juice to taste	

1 Core tomatoes and slice off tops. Scoop out most of flesh and reserve for other uses. Season inside of tomatoes well.

2 Place shrimp, shallot, parsley and celery in bowl. Add mayonnaise and mustard; mix well. Season and add lemon juice to taste.

3 Stuff tomatoes with shrimp salad. Place tomatoes on serving platter or dinner plates and surround with watercress. Drizzle vinaigrette over watercress and serve.

Baked Beet Salad
(4 servings)

5	large beets, cleaned	5
1/2	red onion, finely chopped	1/2
1 tbsp	chopped fresh parsley	15 mL
1 tsp	chopped fresh tarragon	5 mL
2 tbsp	Dijon mustard	30 mL
1	blanched garlic clove, puréed	1
1	shallot, peeled and chopped	1
1/3 cup	heavy cream	75 mL
	juice of 1 lemon	
	salt and freshly ground pepper	

1 Preheat oven to 375°F (190°C).

2 Place beets in baking pan. Cook 40 minutes in oven or adjust time according to size. Test if beets are cooked by inserting paring knife, the same way you would for potatoes. Flesh should be soft with no resistance.

3 Let beets cool, then peel and slice. Cut slices into julienne and place in bowl. Season beets generously. Add onion and herbs to bowl.

4 Mix remaining ingredients together in small bowl and season well. Pour dressing over salad and toss.

5 Serve with fresh asparagus and garnish with lemon quarters and fresh tarragon, if desired.

Salad of Fresh Beets and Endives
(4 to 6 servings)

2	beets, boiled and peeled	2
1	large apple, cored and peeled	1
3	Belgian endives, cored and cleaned	3
2	large boiled potatoes, peeled	2
1 tbsp	chopped fresh parsley	15 mL
1 tbsp	chopped fresh chives	15 mL
1/3 cup	mayonnaise	75 mL
	salt and pepper	
	pinch of paprika	

1 Cut beets and apple into julienne. Place in large bowl.

2 Tear endive leaves into small pieces and add to bowl.

3 Cut potatoes into cubes, add to bowl and toss ingredients.

4 Add fresh herbs, mayonnaise and seasonings. Mix well, correct seasoning and serve.

Cold Purée of Eggplant Salad
(4 servings)

2	eggplants	2
²/₃ cup	olive oil	150 mL
¹/₃ cup	balsamic vinegar	75 mL
¹/₂ tsp	English mustard	2 mL
	salt and freshly ground pepper	
	lemon juice to taste	
	lettuce leaves	

1 Preheat oven to 350°F (180°C).

2 Place whole eggplants in roasting pan. Bake 40 minutes or adjust time according to size. Test if eggplants are done by piercing with paring knife. Flesh should be soft, with no resistance.

3 When cooked, remove eggplants from oven and let cool. Peel and discard skin and purée flesh.

4 Add oil, vinegar and mustard. Mix well and season generously. Add lemon juice to taste.

5 Serve cold on lettuce leaves. Garnish with endives, if desired.

Lamb Salad with Roasted Bell Peppers
(4 to 6 servings)

1	red bell pepper	1
1	yellow pepper	1
1 lb	leftover roast lamb, in julienne	450 g
1	celery stalk, thinly sliced	1
2	hard-boiled eggs, cut in wedges	2
3	bamboo shoots, sliced	3
⅓ cup	Ranch Dressing (see p. 95)	75 mL
¼ cup	toasted pine nuts	50 mL
	salt and pepper	
	lemon juice to taste	

1 Cut bell peppers in half and remove seeds. Oil skin and place cut-side-down on cookie sheet; broil 6 minutes in oven. Remove from oven and let cool. Peel off skin, slice peppers and place in large bowl.

2 Add lamb, celery, hard-boiled eggs and bamboo shoots to bowl. Season well and toss gently.

3 Add Ranch Dressing and mix well. Add lemon juice to taste and season with pepper. Mix again.

4 Serve salad on lettuce leaves and sprinkle with toasted pine nuts.

Fresh Seafood Salad
(4 servings)

1	head Boston lettuce, washed and dried	1
2	tomatoes, peeled, seeded and diced	2
1	apple, cored, peeled and diced	1
1	cucumber, peeled, seeded and diced	1
1 ½ cups	cooked fresh crabmeat	375 mL
6	fresh shrimp, cooked	6
¼ cup	mayonnaise	50 mL
2 tbsp	sour cream	30 mL
1 tbsp	chopped fresh chives	15 mL
	salt and pepper	
	juice of 1 lemon	

1 Divide lettuce leaves among dinner plates. Set aside.

2 Place tomatoes, apple, cucumber and crabmeat in bowl. Peel, devein and cut cooked shrimp in half. Add to bowl and season well.

3 Combine remaining ingredients in small bowl. Add to seafood and mix well. Season to taste.

4 Spoon seafood salad onto plates lined with lettuce leaves. Accompany with radishes, if in season. Garnish with tomato wedges and mâche, if desired.

Avocado, Grapefruit and Smoked Salmon Salad

(4 servings)

2	grapefruits	2
2	avocados, pitted, peeled and diced	2
½ lb	smoked salmon, sliced	225 g
1 tbsp	Dijon mustard	15 mL
¼ cup	olive oil	50 mL
	salt and freshly ground pepper	
	juice of 1½ lemons	
	romaine lettuce leaves	

1 Cut thin slice from top and bottom of grapefruits. Use sharp knife to remove rind and white pith, tracing contour of fruit. Hold fruit in one hand and cut between membranes to release sections of fruit. Place in bowl.

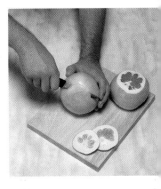

2 Add avocados and smoked salmon to bowl. Season generously with salt and pepper.

3 Mix mustard, lemon juice, salt, pepper and oil together in separate bowl. Taste and add more oil if lemon is too strong.

4 Pour vinaigrette over salad, toss gently and serve on lettuce leaves.

Mâche and Escarole Salad
(4 servings)

1	head escarole endive	1
1	head curly endive	1
1	head mâche	1
⅓ cup	heavy cream	75 mL
1 tbsp	Dijon mustard	15 mL
	salt and freshly ground pepper	
	lemon juice to taste	

1 Wash greens in plenty of cold water and dry thoroughly. Tear leaves into small pieces and place in large bowl.

2 Mix cream and mustard together; season well. Add lemon juice to taste and pour dressing over greens. Toss and serve.

Roquefort Salad
(4 servings)

2	heads romaine lettuce, washed and dried	2
5	slices crisp-cooked bacon	5
½ lb	Roquefort cheese, crumbled	225 g
2 tbsp	wine vinegar	30 mL
⅓ cup	olive oil	75 mL
1½ cups	croûtons	375 mL
	salt and freshly ground pepper	
	juice of ½ lemon	
	few drops of Worcestershire sauce	

1 Tear lettuce leaves into small pieces and place in large bowl. Season generously. Chop bacon and toss with lettuce.

2 Place three quarters of cheese in food processor. Add vinegar, oil, salt and pepper. Blend several seconds. Add lemon juice and Worcestershire sauce; blend again to combine.

3 Pour dressing over salad and mix well. Add remaining cheese and croûtons. Toss and serve. Garnish with cherry tomatoes and parsley, if desired.

Salad Isabella
(4 to 6 servings)

½ lb	fresh mushrooms, cleaned and thinly sliced	225 g
2	celery stalks from celery heart	2
2	boiled potatoes, peeled	2
½ lb	green beans, pared and cooked	225 g
3	cooked artichoke bottoms, in julienne	3
1 tbsp	chopped fresh parsley	15 mL
	salt and pepper	
	Mustard Vinaigrette (see p. 86)	

Mustard Vinaigrette (see p. 86)

1 Place mushrooms in large bowl.

2 Slice celery stalks and potatoes into julienne. Add to bowl containing mushrooms.

3 Cut green beans into 1-in (2.5-cm) pieces. Add to bowl with artichoke bottoms and parsley. Season well.

4 Pour vinaigrette over salad and mix well. Serve.

Romaine Salad with Warm Bacon Dressing

(4 to 6 servings)

5 tbsp	olive oil	75 mL
5	slices bacon, diced	5
1	red onion, peeled and sliced in rings	1
1	large head romaine lettuce, washed and dried	1
12	cherry tomatoes, halved	12
2	garlic cloves, peeled and thinly sliced	2
2 tbsp	balsamic vinegar	30 mL
¼ cup	grated Parmesan cheese	50 mL
	salt and freshly ground pepper	

1 Heat 1 tbsp (15 mL) oil in frying pan over medium heat. Add bacon and cook until crisp. Using slotted spoon, remove bacon and set aside.

2 Add red onion to hot bacon fat in pan. Cook 5 minutes over medium heat.

3 Tear lettuce into small pieces and place in large bowl. Add red onion and bacon. Pour in some of hot bacon fat. Toss quickly.

4 Add tomatoes, garlic and vinegar; mix well. Season generously and add remaining oil. Mix well and add cheese. Toss and serve.

German Potato Salad with Apple
(4 to 6 servings)

2	hard-boiled eggs	2
1 tbsp	Dijon mustard	15 mL
1	shallot, peeled and chopped	1
3 tbsp	wine vinegar	45 mL
5 tbsp	olive oil	75 mL
2 cups	diced cooked potatoes	500 mL
2 cups	diced peeled apples	500 mL
3	gherkins, in julienne	3
1 tbsp	chopped fresh parsley	15 mL
	salt and freshly ground pepper	

1 Slice hard-boiled eggs in half and place yolks in bowl. Chop egg whites and set aside.

2 Mash egg yolks with spoon. Incorporate mustard, shallot and vinegar. When combined, add oil and mix well. Season with salt and pepper.

3 Place potatoes, apple and gherkins in separate bowl. Add egg dressing and mix well. Add parsley and season generously; mix again.

4 Serve salad on lettuce leaves and decorate with chopped egg whites.

Warm Scallop and Shrimp Salad
(4 servings)

4	garlic cloves, peeled, crushed and puréed	4
2	anchovy fillets, drained and puréed	2
⅓ cup	olive oil	75 mL
12	fresh shrimp, peeled, deveined and halved	12
I cup	croûtons	250 mL
12	fresh large scallops, cleaned and halved	12
I	large head romaine lettuce, washed and dried	I
3 tbsp	grated Parmesan cheese	45 mL
	juice of I lemon	
	salt and pepper	

1 Place half of puréed garlic in bowl with anchovies; mix well. Add lemon juice and mix again. Add half of oil, season and blend well. Set aside.

2 Heat remaining oil in frying pan over medium heat. Add shrimp and croûtons; cook 2 minutes. Add scallops and remaining garlic; continue cooking 3 minutes.

3 Meanwhile, tear lettuce leaves into small pieces and place in large bowl. Arrange shrimp and scallop mixture over lettuce. Add lemon vinaigrette and mix well.

4 Season, sprinkle with cheese and serve.

Citrus Fruit Salad with Avocado
(4 servings)

2	large ripe avocados	2
2	large grapefruits	2
3	oranges	3
⅓ cup	heavy cream	75 mL
1 tbsp	sour cream	15 mL
1 tsp	Dijon mustard	5 mL
	juice of ½ lemon	
	salt and white pepper	
	cayenne pepper to taste	
	fresh mint leaves	

1 Cut avocados in half, lengthwise. Twist halves apart and remove pit. Peel and slice flesh and place in bowl.

2 Cut thin slice from top and bottom of grapefruits and oranges. Use sharp knife to remove rind and white pith, tracing contour of fruit. Hold fruit in one hand and cut between membranes to release sections of fruit. Add to bowl containing avocados.

3 Mix heavy cream with sour cream. Stir in mustard and lemon juice. Season with salt and both peppers.

4 Pour dressing over salad and mix well. Garnish portions with fresh mint leaves.

Marinated Tomato and Red Onion Salad

(4 servings)

1	yellow bell pepper	1
4	large tomatoes, cored	4
1	red onion, peeled and sliced very thinly	1
1 tsp	chopped fresh ginger	5 mL
¼ tsp	ground ginger	1 mL
2	garlic cloves, peeled and thinly sliced	2
	salt and freshly ground pepper	
	lemon juice	
	chopped chili pepper to taste	

1 Cut bell pepper in half and remove seeds. Oil skin and place cut-side-down on cookie sheet; broil 6 minutes in oven. Remove from oven and let cool. Peel off skin, slice pepper and set aside.

2 Plunge tomatoes in saucepan with boiling water. Remove tomatoes after 1 minute or as soon as skins start to loosen. When cool enough to handle, peel off skins. Cut tomatoes in quarters and squeeze out seeds.

3 Place tomatoes in bowl and add onion; season well. Toss and set aside.

4 Place lemon juice, fresh and ground ginger and garlic in small bowl. Add chopped chili pepper to taste and mix well.

5 Pour mixture over tomatoes and mix well. Marinate 2 hours at room temperature.

6 Serve marinated salad decorated with slices of roasted bell pepper.

Fresh Fennel Salad
(4 servings)

1	large fennel bulb	1
4 tbsp	olive oil	60 mL
6	cooked artichoke hearts, halved	6
3 tbsp	lemon juice	45 mL
	salt and freshly ground pepper	

1 Remove leaves and stem from fennel bulb. Cut in half and peel. Cut each half, lengthwise, into 3 pieces.

2 Place fennel in saucepan and pour in enough water to barely cover. Add 1 tbsp (15 mL) oil and season with salt. Cover and cook 30 minutes over low heat. When cooked, remove pan from stove and let fennel cool.

3 Place fennel and artichoke hearts on platter. Mix lemon juice with remaining oil and season well. Pour over salad. Garnish with spinach leaves, cherry tomatoes and fresh fennel, if desired.

Spring Salad with Lemon Dressing
(4 to 6 servings)

1	head romaine lettuce, washed and dried	1
1	head leaf lettuce, washed and dried	1
½ lb	fresh mushrooms*, cleaned, sliced and blanched	225 g
¾ lb	fresh asparagus, cooked and cut in 1-in (2.5-cm) pieces	350 g
12	radishes, cleaned and quartered	12
¼ cup	heavy cream	50 mL
2 tbsp	mayonnaise	30 mL
½ tsp	Dijon mustard	2 mL
1 tsp	grated lemon rind	5 mL
	salt and pepper	
	juice of 1 lemon	

1 Tear lettuce leaves into small pieces and place in large bowl. Add mushrooms, asparagus and radishes. Season well.

2 Place cream, mayonnaise and mustard in small bowl. Mix together and season well. Add lemon rind and lemon juice; mix again.

3 Pour dressing over salad and toss. Correct seasoning and serve. Decorate salad with slices of hard-boiled egg, if desired.

*You may use whichever mushrooms are in season: shiitake, oyster, etc.

Russian Salad
(4 to 6 servings)

3	carrots, pared and diced	3
3	potatoes, peeled and diced	3
1	small white turnip, peeled and diced	1
1 cup	frozen green peas	250 mL
½ lb	green beans, pared	225 g
1 cup	mayonnaise	250 mL
1 tbsp	chopped fresh parsley	15 mL
1 tbsp	chopped fresh chives	15 mL
	salt and pepper	
	lemon juice to taste	
	few drops of hot pepper sauce	

1 Cook all vegetables in salted, boiling water until tender. Drain thoroughly and place in bowl.

2 Season vegetables well and incorporate mayonnaise. Add lemon juice to taste and mix well.

3 Add fresh herbs and hot pepper sauce. Mix and correct seasoning.

4 Chill salad before serving.

Caesar Salad
(4 to 6 servings)

2	large heads romaine lettuce	2
1	garlic clove, peeled and halved	1
2	blanched garlic cloves, puréed	2
6	anchovy fillets, drained and puréed	6
4 tbsp	olive oil	60 mL
1	large egg, coddled 2 minutes	1
1 1/2 cups	croûtons	375 mL
1/2 cup	grated Parmesan cheese	125 mL
	juice of 2 lemons	
	salt and freshly ground pepper	

1 Separate lettuce into leaves and wash well in plenty of cold water. Drain and dry thoroughly. Tear leaves into small pieces and set aside.

2 Rub inside of wooden salad bowl with garlic halves. Discard garlic.

3 Place puréed garlic in salad bowl. Add anchovies and mix together. Mix in oil. Add lemon juice, season and mix well. Add coddled egg and incorporate with whisk.

4 Add lettuce to dressing in bowl. Toss until evenly coated. Season well and toss again.

5 Add croûtons and cheese. Toss, season and serve.

Cucumber and Shrimp Salad
(4 servings)

¾ lb	fresh shrimp	350 g
1	head Boston lettuce, washed and dried	1
1	large cucumber, peeled, seeded and sliced	1
1 tbsp	chopped fresh chives	15 mL
1	shallot, peeled and chopped	1
4 tbsp	extra virgin olive oil	60 mL
1 tsp	chopped chili pepper	5 mL
	salt and pepper	

1 Place shrimp in saucepan with cold water and bring to boil. Remove pan from heat and let shrimp stand 3 minutes. Place pan under cold running water to stop cooking process. Drain shrimp and peel. Using tip of paring knife, remove dark dorsal vein.

2 Arrange lettuce leaves on serving plates.

3 Place shrimp in large bowl. Add remaining ingredients and mix well. Season to taste and serve over lettuce.

Lettuce and Carrot Salad with Chèvre
(4 servings)

1	head romaine lettuce, washed and dried	1
2	carrots, pared and grated	2
1	apple, cored, peeled and diced large	1
2 tbsp	olive oil	30 mL
3 oz	chèvre (goats' milk) cheese	90 g
	juice of 1 ½ lemons	
	salt and pepper	

1 Tear lettuce into small pieces and place in bowl. Add carrots and apple. Squeeze in lemon juice and mix well.

2 Season generously and pour in oil; mix again. Add chèvre cheese, mix gently and serve.

3 Accompany with garlic bread, if desired.

Cucumber and Egg Salad
(4 to 6 servings)

3	cucumbers, sliced	3
1 tbsp	chopped fresh parsley	15 mL
2	hard-boiled eggs, chopped	2
	salt	
	olive oil and wine vinegar to taste	
	freshly ground pepper	
	radiccio leaves (optional)	

1 Spread cucumber slices on large serving platter. Sprinkle generously with salt and let stand 2 hours at room temperature. Rinse cucumbers under cold water and drain well.

2 Place cucumbers in deep serving platter. Add oil and vinegar to taste. Sprinkle with parsley and season with pepper.

3 Decorate center of platter with radiccio leaves and hard-boiled egg. Serve.

Simple Avocado Salad with Sesame Seeds
(4 servings)

2 tbsp	wine vinegar	30 mL
1 tbsp	Dijon mustard	15 mL
6 tbsp	olive oil	90 mL
2	garlic cloves, peeled and halved	2
2	large ripe avocados	2
2 tbsp	toasted sesame seeds	30 mL
	lemon juice	
	red leaf lettuce leaves	

1 Place vinegar and mustard in bowl. Season well and add oil. Whisk together. Add garlic and let stand 15 minutes.

2 Meanwhile, cut avocados in half, lengthwise. Twist halves apart and remove pit. Peel and slice flesh. Toss in lemon juice and arrange slices on lettuce leaves.

3 Remove garlic from vinaigrette and discard. Whisk in toasted sesame seeds and drizzle vinaigrette over avocados. Garnish with radiccio leaves and enoki mushrooms, if desired.

Quick Navy Bean and Lentil Salad

(4 to 6 servings)

1	red bell pepper	1
½ cup	canned navy beans, drained	125 mL
½ cup	canned lentils, drained	125 mL
½	red onion, thinly sliced	½
3 tbsp	red wine vinegar	45 mL
4 tbsp	olive oil	60 mL
1 tbsp	chopped fresh tarragon	15 mL
	salt and pepper	

1 Cut bell pepper in half and remove seeds. Oil skin and place cut-side-down on cookie sheet; broil 6 minutes in oven. Remove from oven and let cool. Peel off skin, slice pepper and place in large bowl.

2 Add navy beans, lentils and red onion. Toss together.

3 Add remaining ingredients and mix well. Marinate 30 minutes at room temperature.

4 Add more oil or vinegar as desired, before serving.

Hot Lentil Salad with Bacon Dressing
(4 to 6 servings)

1 tbsp	olive oil	15 mL
5	slices bacon, diced	5
½	red onion, coarsely chopped	½
2	tomatoes, peeled, seeded and chopped (see p. 7)	2
1	garlic clove, peeled and sliced	1
3 tbsp	wine vinegar	45 mL
2 cups	cooked lentils, still warm	500 mL
1 tbsp	chopped fresh basil	15 mL
3 tbsp	olive oil	45 mL
	salt and pepper	

1 Heat 1 tbsp (15 mL) oil in frying pan over medium heat. Add bacon and onion; cook until crisp. Transfer contents of pan to bowl.

2 Add tomatoes and garlic to hot pan. Continue cooking 3 minutes over medium heat. Pour in vinegar and cook 1 minute over high heat.

3 Add lentils to bacon and onion in bowl. Pour in hot dressing and mix well. Add remaining ingredients and mix again.

4 Correct seasoning and serve with garlic cheese bread, if desired.

Shrimp and Snow Peas with Mixed Greens
(4 servings)

1 tbsp	soy sauce	15 mL
2 tbsp	dry white wine	30 mL
1 tsp	sesame oil	5 mL
1	garlic clove, peeled, crushed and chopped	1
2 tbsp	olive oil	30 mL
16	shrimp, peeled and deveined	16
2	garlic cloves, peeled and thinly sliced	2
⅓ lb	snow peas, pared	150 g
1	small head radiccio, washed and dried	1
1	small bunch watercress, washed and dried	1
3	Belgian endives, cored, washed and dried	3
	pinch of sugar	
	salt and pepper	

1 Mix soy sauce with white wine and sesame oil. Add chopped garlic and pinch of sugar. Mix again and set aside.

2 Heat olive oil in frying pan over medium heat. Add shrimp and sliced garlic; season well. Cook 3 minutes over high heat, stirring once. Remove shrimp from pan and set aside in large bowl.

3 Add snow peas to hot pan and season well. Cook 3 minutes over high heat. Add to shrimp in bowl.

4 Add radiccio leaves, watercress and endives to bowl. Season generously and pour in soy dressing. Toss and serve with garlic bread, if desired.

Mixed Summer Vegetable Salad
(4 to 6 servings)

1	small head broccoli, in florets	1
1	small head cauliflower, in florets	1
½ lb	green beans, pared	225 g
1	bunch fresh asparagus, pared	1
1	carrot, pared and sliced	1
⅓ cup	mayonnaise	75 mL
¼ cup	Ranch Dressing (see p. 95)	50 mL
10	slices salami, in julienne	10
1 tbsp	chopped fresh basil	15 mL
1 tbsp	chopped fresh tarragon	15 mL
	salt and pepper	

1 Blanch vegetables separately in salted, boiling water until just tender. Drain well.

2 Place blanched vegetables in large bowl and season well. Add mayonnaise and Ranch Dressing; mix well.

3 Add salami and fresh herbs. Mix lightly and serve.

Shrimp and Litchi Nut Salad
(4 servings)

1 ½ lb	fresh shrimp, cooked, peeled and deveined	700 g
2	ripe avocados, peeled, pitted and sliced	2
1 cup	litchi nuts	250 mL
2	garlic cloves, peeled and sliced	2
2 tbsp	lemon juice	30 mL
2 tbsp	tarragon vinegar	30 mL
7 tbsp	olive oil	105 mL
1 tbsp	chili sauce	15 mL
	lettuce leaves	
	salt and freshly ground pepper	
	pinch of sugar	
	pinch of English mustard	
	pinch of paprika	
	lemon wedges	

1 Arrange lettuce leaves on serving platter. Fill platter with shrimp and slices of avocado. Top with litchi nuts. Season well.

2 Place garlic, lemon juice, vinegar, oil and chili sauce in small bowl. Mix well. Add all seasonings and mix again.

3 Drizzle sauce over shrimp and avocados. Garnish with lemon wedges and serve.

Fancy Tuna Salad
(4 to 6 servings)

¾ lb	fresh tuna, poached and flaked	350 g
1	small cucumber, peeled, seeded and diced	1
1	celery stalk, diced	1
3	green onions, chopped	3
4 tbsp	chopped pimiento pepper	60 mL
2	tomatoes, peeled, seeded and chopped	2
4 tbsp	mayonnaise	60 mL
1 tbsp	Dijon mustard	15 mL
1 tbsp	chopped fresh parsley	15 mL
4	hard-boiled eggs, quartered	4
	salt and pepper	
	juice of 1 lemon	
	lettuce leaves	

1 Place tuna, cucumber, celery, green onions, pimiento pepper and tomatoes in bowl. Season with salt and pepper.

2 Mix mayonnaise with mustard in separate bowl. Add to salad and mix well.

3 Add parsley and lemon juice; mix again. Correct seasoning and serve salad on lettuce leaves. Garnish with hard-boiled eggs.

Warm Cucumber Potato Salad with Brie Cheese
(4 servings)

2	cucumbers, peeled, seeded and sliced	2
2	large potatoes	2
½	red onion, peeled and sliced in rings	½
1	small head romaine lettuce, washed and dried	1
3 tbsp	red wine vinegar	45 mL
1 tbsp	chopped fresh parsley	15 mL
1 tbsp	chopped fresh chives	15 mL
4 tbsp	olive oil	60 mL
10	small slices of Brie cheese	10
	salt and pepper	

1 Spread sliced cucumbers on large platter. Sprinkle with salt and let stand 30 minutes at room temperature. Pour off liquid, rinse under cold water and drain well.

2 Meanwhile, boil potatoes in skins until cooked. Peel potatoes, slice and place in large bowl.

3 Add cucumbers and onion to potatoes. Tear lettuce leaves into small pieces and add to bowl. Season well.

4 Sprinkle in vinegar and fresh herbs. Toss, then pour in oil. Mix well. Correct seasoning and garnish portions with Brie cheese.

Tropical Fruit and Chicken Salad
(4 to 6 servings)

1	ripe pineapple	1
1	orange	1
1	grapefruit	1
1	thick slice watermelon, diced	1
2	whole chicken breasts, cooked* and sliced	2
¼ cup	mayonnaise	50 mL
2 tbsp	sour cream	30 mL
	salt and freshly ground pepper	
	dash of paprika and cayenne pepper	

1 To prepare pineapple, slice off frond and stem end. Cut pineapple lengthwise into quarters. Remove core from each quarter and discard. Cut off rind from quarters and dice flesh.

2 Cut thin slice from top and bottom of orange and grapefruit. Use sharp knife to remove rind and white pith, tracing contour of fruit. Hold fruit in one hand and cut between membranes to release sections of fruit.

3 Place all ingredients in bowl and toss together. Cover and marinate 1 hour in refrigerator.

4 Serve on romaine lettuce leaves and decorate with whole slices of lime and orange, if desired.

*Chicken may be broiled or barbecued.

Spicy Bell Pepper Salad with Chickpeas
(4 to 6 servings)

1	red bell pepper	1
1	yellow bell pepper	1
1	green bell pepper	1
1 cup	canned chickpeas, drained	250 mL
2	garlic cloves, peeled and thinly sliced	2
1 tbsp	wine vinegar	15 mL
3 tbsp	olive oil	45 mL
	salt and freshly ground pepper	
	crushed chilies to taste	
	juice of 1 lemon	

1 Cut bell peppers in half and remove seeds. Oil skin and place cut-side-down on cookie sheet; broil 6 minutes in oven. Remove from oven and let cool. Peel off skin, slice peppers and place in large bowl.

2 Add chickpeas and season well. Add remaining ingredients and mix well. Marinate 30 minutes before serving.

Classic Garden Tomato Salad
(4 to 6 servings)

5	ripe tomatoes*	5
2	shallots, peeled and finely chopped	2
1 tbsp	chopped fresh parsley	15 mL
	olive oil and red wine vinegar to taste	
	salt and freshly ground pepper	

1 Core tomatoes and cut into quarters. Place on large serving platter. Season generously with salt and pepper.

2 Sprinkle shallots and parsley over tomatoes. Add oil and vinegar to taste; mix well. Correct seasoning and marinate 30 minutes at room temperature. Add more oil and vinegar, if needed.

3 Serve at room temperature.

*You may also use yellow tomatoes, in season.

Steak and Beans in Salad
(4 servings)

2 tbsp	red wine vinegar	30 mL
1 tbsp	Dijon mustard	15 mL
1	garlic clove, peeled, crushed and chopped	1
1 tbsp	chopped fresh tarragon	15 mL
$^{1}/_{2}$ cup	olive oil	125 mL
$^{1}/_{2}$ lb	leftover cooked sirloin steak, sliced $^{1}/_{2}$ in (1 cm) thick	225 g
1 $^{1}/_{2}$ cups	cooked white beans	375 mL
1	red leaf lettuce, washed and dried	1
2	hard-boiled eggs, sliced	2
	salt and pepper	
	chopped fresh parsley	

1 Place vinegar, mustard, salt and pepper in small bowl. Add garlic, tarragon and oil; whisk to incorporate.

2 Place beef and beans in separate bowl. Season generously and pour in dressing. Mix well, cover and marinate 1 hour in refrigerator.

3 To serve salad, line plates with lettuce leaves. Add portions of beef and bean salad and decorate with sliced hard-boiled eggs. Sprinkle with chopped parsley and serve.

Rice Salad with Raisins and Toasted Nuts
(6 to 8 servings)

2 cups	steamed white rice	500 mL
1/2 cup	pitted black olives, chopped	125 mL
1/4 cup	diced pimiento pepper	50 mL
1/2 cup	cooked green peas	125 mL
1/2 cup	sliced celery	125 mL
1/2 cup	golden seedless raisins	125 mL
1/2 cup	toasted pine nuts	125 mL
1/2 cup	Basic Vinaigrette (see p. 89)	125 mL
4	hard-boiled eggs	4
1/3 cup	mayonnaise	75 mL
	salt and pepper	
	cayenne pepper	
	lemon juice	
	fresh parsley sprigs	

1 Place rice, olives, pimiento pepper and green peas in large bowl. Add celery, raisins and pine nuts.

2 Season generously with salt, pepper and cayenne pepper. Pour in vinaigrette and toss well. Mix in lemon juice to taste.

3 Spoon salad onto dinner plates. Slice hard-boiled eggs carefully. Arrange slices overlapping on rice salad. Add dollop of mayonnaise. Decorate plates with parsley sprigs and serve.

Hot Chicken Salad with Raspberry Vinaigrette
(4 servings)

1	large head romaine lettuce, washed and dried	1
1	head radiccio, washed and dried	1
¼ cup	olive oil	50 mL
2	garlic cloves, peeled, crushed and chopped	2
2	shallots, peeled and chopped	2
1	whole chicken breast, cooked and thinly sliced	1
2 tbsp	raspberry wine vinegar	30 mL
1 ½ cups	croûtons	375 mL
¼ cup	toasted pine nuts	50 mL
1 tbsp	chopped fresh basil	15 mL
1 tbsp	chopped fresh parsley	15 mL
	salt and pepper	
	lemon juice to taste	

1 Tear romaine and radiccio leaves into small pieces and arrange on serving platter.

2 Heat 2 tbsp (30 mL) oil in frying pan over medium heat. Add garlic, shallots and sliced chicken. Season and cook 2 minutes over high heat.

3 Add vinegar, mix well and cook 1 minute over low heat. Place over lettuce.

4 Add remaining oil to pan. When hot, add croûtons, pine nuts and herbs. Cook 2 minutes over high heat. Add to salad.

5 Season salad well and sprinkle with lemon juice. Serve.

Celeriac Rémoulade
(4 servings)

I	celeriac	I
¾ cup	mayonnaise	175 mL
I tsp	Dijon mustard	5 mL
I tbsp	chopped fresh parsley	15 mL
I tsp	basil	5 mL
I	gherkin, in julienne	I
2 tbsp	capers	30 mL
	salt and pepper	

1 Place celeriac in salted, boiling water. Blanch 6 minutes or adjust time according to size. Remove celeriac, peel and cut in fine julienne.

2 Place celeriac in bowl with remaining ingredients. Mix together and correct seasoning.

3 Serve on greens of your choice (e.g. lettuce, mâche, red endive) and accompany with Italian salami, if desired.

Cauliflower and Avocado Salad
(4 to 6 servings)

1	cauliflower	1
3	beets, boiled, peeled and sliced	3
1	avocado, peeled, halved, pitted and sliced	1
	salt and pepper	
	Tomato Vinaigrette (see p. 90)	

1 Wash cauliflower and remove dark leaves at stem end. Place cauliflower, core-side-down, in pot with salted, boiling water. Blanch 5 minutes. Drain and cool under cold water.

2 Divide cauliflower into florets and place in salad bowl. Add beets and avocado; season well.

3 Pour in Tomato Vinaigrette and mix well. Marinate 30 minutes at room temperature before serving.

Brittany Salad
(4 to 6 servings)

2	**zucchini**	2
3	**large tomatoes, cored**	3
4	**cooked artichoke bottoms, sliced**	4
½ lb	**fresh shrimp, peeled, deveined and cooked (see technique)**	225 g
2	**hard-boiled eggs, sliced**	2
	salt and freshly ground pepper	
	Mustard Vinaigrette (see p. 86)	
	lettuce leaves	

1 Cut zucchini into slices ½ in (1 cm) thick. Cook 2 minutes in salted, boiling water. Remove using slotted spoon and set aside to drain. Pat dry with paper towels.

2 Plunge tomatoes in boiling water just long enough to loosen skins. Remove, let cool and peel. Cut tomatoes in wedges.

3 Place all vegetables and shrimp in large bowl; season well. Pour in vinaigrette and mix well. Correct seasoning.

4 Serve salad on lettuce leaves and decorate with slices of hard-boiled egg.

Picnic Salad
(4 to 6 servings)

2	boiled potatoes, peeled and diced	2
1 ½ cups	cooked white beans	375 mL
½ cup	pitted black olives	125 mL
2	garlic cloves, peeled, crushed and chopped	2
1 tbsp	wine vinegar	15 mL
4 tbsp	olive oil	60 mL
¾ cup	canned tuna, drained and flaked	175 mL
1 tbsp	chopped fresh basil	15 mL
1 tbsp	chopped fresh parsley	15 mL
	salt and freshly ground pepper	
	juice of 1 lemon	
	radiccio, washed and dried	

1 Place potatoes, white beans, olives and garlic in large bowl. Season generously. Add lemon juice and vinegar; mix well.

2 Pour in oil and mix well. Add tuna and fresh herbs; mix again. Correct seasoning and serve on bed of radiccio.

Cucumber and Bocconcini Cheese Salad

(4 to 6 servings)

3	cucumbers, peeled, seeded and diced	3
½ lb	Bocconcini cheese, cubed	225 g
3	green onions, chopped	3
12	radishes, cleaned and sliced	12
¾ cup	sour cream	175 mL
1 tbsp	tarragon vinegar	15 mL
2 tbsp	chopped dill pickle	30 mL
1 tsp	Dijon mustard	5 mL
2	blanched garlic cloves, puréed	2
1 tbsp	extra virgin olive oil	15 mL
	salt and pepper	
	pinch of paprika	

1 Spread diced cucumbers on large platter. Sprinkle with salt and let stand 2 hours at room temperature. Pour off liquid, rinse under cold water and drain well.

2 Place cucumbers in bowl with cheese, green onions and radishes. Season well, cover and refrigerate 1 hour.

3 Mix remaining ingredients together in small bowl. Add to salad and mix well. Correct seasoning and serve.

Mediterranean Pasta Salad

(4 to 6 servings)

3	blanched garlic cloves, puréed	3
1 tbsp	Dijon mustard	15 mL
2 tbsp	balsamic vinegar	30 mL
6 tbsp	olive oil	90 mL
¾ lb	pasta, cooked	350 g
¼ cup	sun-dried tomatoes, chopped	50 mL
4	cooked artichoke hearts, quartered	4
1 cup	cooked white beans	250 mL
12	slices Italian salami, in julienne	12
3 oz	mozzarella cheese, diced	90 g
	salt and freshly ground pepper	
	fresh chopped herbs in season	

1 Place garlic and mustard in small bowl; season well. Add vinegar and mix well. Whisk in oil and correct seasoning.

2 Place pasta, sun-dried tomatoes, artichoke hearts and white beans in large bowl. Pour in dressing and mix well. Season generously.

3 Add salami and cheese; mix again. Sprinkle with chopped fresh herbs in season and serve.

Chickpeas with Julienne of Salami
(4 to 6 servings)

2 cups	canned chickpeas, drained	500 mL
5	slices salami, cut in julienne	5
½ cup	pitted black olives	125 mL
½	green bell pepper, thinly sliced	½
2	green onions, chopped	2
¼ cup	chopped pimiento pepper	50 mL
1 tbsp	olive oil	15 mL
	salt and pepper	
	few drops of Tabasco sauce	
	juice of 1 large lemon	

1 Place all ingredients, except oil and lemon juice, in large bowl.

2 Mix in oil and lemon juice. Correct seasoning, cover and marinate 2 hours in refrigerator.

3 Serve salad on lettuce leaves. Garnish with lemon slices and fresh sage, if desired.

Wilted Greens in Salad
(4 servings)

1	head romaine lettuce, washed and dried	1
1	head escarole endive, washed and dried	1
1 tbsp	olive oil	15 mL
5	slices bacon	5
1	red onion, peeled and sliced in rings	1
1	red bell pepper, thinly sliced	1
2	tomatoes, peeled, seeded and cubed	2
2	garlic cloves, peeled and thinly sliced	2
3 tbsp	catsup	45 mL
1 tbsp	Dijon mustard	15 mL
	salt and freshly ground pepper	
	few drops hot pepper sauce	
	juice of 1 lemon	

1 Tear greens into small pieces and place in large bowl.

2 Heat oil in frying pan over medium heat. Add bacon and cook until crisp. Remove bacon from pan and set aside to drain on paper towels.

3 Add red onion rings to hot pan and cook 4 minutes over high heat. Add bell pepper, tomatoes and garlic; continue cooking 2 minutes.

4 Pour hot vegetables over greens and toss quickly; season well. Crumble bacon and sprinkle over salad.

5 Mix catsup and mustard together. Add hot pepper sauce and lemon juice. Pour over salad, toss and serve.

Warm Chicken Liver Salad

(4 servings)

1	large head leaf lettuce, washed and dried	1
1/3 cup	olive oil	75 mL
3	slices bacon, diced	3
1/2 lb	chicken livers, cleaned and sliced	225 g
2	garlic cloves, peeled, crushed and chopped	2
2	shallots, peeled and chopped	2
2 tbsp	balsamic vinegar	30 mL
1 tbsp	chopped fresh chives	15 mL
1 1/2 cups	croûtons	375 mL
	salt and freshly ground pepper	

1 Tear lettuce leaves into small pieces and place in large bowl.

2 Heat 1 tbsp (15 mL) oil in frying pan over high heat. Add bacon and cook until crisp. Remove bacon and add to lettuce in bowl.

3 Add half of remaining oil to pan and heat. Add chicken livers and season well. Cook 2 minutes over medium-high heat. Add to salad bowl.

4 Add remaining oil to pan. When hot, add garlic and shallots; cook 1 minute over medium heat. Pour in vinegar and cook 20 seconds.

5 Pour mixture over salad and mix well. Add chives and croûtons. Correct seasoning, toss and serve.

Cold Roast Beef Salad
(4 servings)

1 lb	roast beef, sliced in julienne	450 g
1	red bell pepper, in julienne	1
1	celery stalk, thinly sliced	1
½ lb	green beans, pared, cooked and halved	225 g
1	large tomato, peeled, seeded and cut into julienne	1
1 tbsp	chopped fresh parsley	15 mL
1 tbsp	chopped fresh basil	15 mL
3 tbsp	balsamic vinegar	45 mL
7 tbsp	olive oil	105 mL
	salt and pepper	
	few drops of Tabasco sauce	

1 Place roast beef and vegetables in large bowl. Add fresh herbs and remaining ingredients.

2 Mix well and correct seasoning. Cover and marinate 30 minutes in refrigerator before serving.

3 Serve on lettuce leaves, if desired, and garnish with fresh herbs.

Greek Salad
(4 to 6 servings)

1	large head romaine lettuce, washed and dried	1
1	head red leaf lettuce, washed and dried	1
1	small red onion, peeled and sliced in rings	1
1	green bell pepper, thinly sliced	1
1	red bell pepper, thinly sliced	1
2	tomatoes, cored and cut in wedges	2
½ cup	Greek olives	125 mL
1 cup	cubed feta cheese	250 mL
2 tbsp	wine vinegar	30 mL
2 tbsp	lemon juice	30 mL
2	garlic cloves, peeled, crushed and chopped	2
1 tsp	oregano	5 mL
⅓ cup	olive oil	75 mL
	salt and freshly ground pepper	
	fresh herbs in season	

1 Tear lettuce leaves into small pieces and place in large bowl. Add red onion, bell peppers, tomatoes, olives and cheese. Season with salt and pepper.

2 Place vinegar, lemon juice, garlic and oregano in small bowl. Season with salt and pepper. Add oil and whisk to incorporate.

3 Pour dressing over salad, mix well and garnish portions with fresh herbs, if desired.

Salad Aida
(4 servings)

1	head curly endive	1
1	head radiccio	1
2	tomatoes, cored and cut in wedges	2
2	cooked artichoke bottoms, sliced	2
1	green bell pepper, sliced	1
	salt and freshly ground pepper	
	Mustard Vinaigrette (see p. 86)	
	lemon juice to taste	

1 Wash endive and radiccio in plenty of cold water. Dry thoroughly and tear leaves into small pieces. Place in large bowl with tomatoes.

2 Add artichoke bottoms and green pepper to bowl. Season well and pour in vinaigrette. Toss and add lemon juice to taste. Mix well, correct seasoning and serve.

Curried Shrimp and Rice Salad
(6 servings)

I cup	long grain rice, rinsed	250 mL
I tbsp	olive oil	15 mL
¾ lb	fresh shrimp, peeled and deveined	350 g
I	red bell pepper, diced	I
I	celery stalk, diced	I
4	slices cantaloupe, peeled and diced	4
I ½ tbsp	curry powder	25 mL
2	blanched garlic cloves, puréed	2
2 tbsp	wine vinegar	30 mL
6 tbsp	olive oil	90 mL
⅓ cup	plain yogurt	75 mL
3 tbsp	chutney	45 mL
	salt and pepper	
	chopped fresh parsley	

1 Steam rice for 40 minutes. Season well and set aside to cool.

2 Heat I tbsp (15 mL) oil in frying pan over medium heat. Add shrimp and cook 4 minutes, stirring during cooking. Add bell pepper and continue cooking I minute.

3 Transfer shrimp and bell pepper to large bowl. Add rice, celery and cantaloupe. Season generously and mix.

4 Place curry powder, garlic, vinegar and remaining oil in small bowl. Season well and whisk together. Pour over salad and mix well.

5 Stir in yogurt and chutney. Correct seasoning, sprinkle with parsley and serve.

Plain Red Cabbage Salad
(4 to 6 servings)

1	head red cabbage, cored and shredded	1
4 tbsp	cider vinegar	60 mL
6 tbsp	olive oil	90 mL
12	black peppercorns	12
	pickling spices	
	salt and pepper	

1 Blanch cabbage 3 minutes in salted, boiling water. Cool under cold, running water and drain well. Place in bowl.

2 Place remaining ingredients in saucepan. Cook 3 minutes over medium heat.

3 Pour hot dressing over cabbage and season generously. If necessary add more oil and vinegar. Marinate 3 hours before serving.

Black Bean Salad
(4 servings)

2 cups	cooked black beans	500 mL
½	red onion, peeled and chopped	½
1	celery stalk, diced	1
2	tomatoes, peeled, seeded and chopped	2
2	garlic cloves, peeled, crushed and chopped	2
1 tbsp	chopped fresh parsley	15 mL
3 tbsp	balsamic vinegar	45 mL
6 tbsp	olive oil	90 mL
1 tbsp	grain mustard	15 mL
	salt and freshly ground pepper	

1 Place beans and vegetables in bowl. Add garlic, parsley and vinegar. Mix well.

2 Add remaining ingredients and mix again. Correct seasoning, cover and marinate 30 minutes in refrigerator before serving.

Tossed Green Salad
(6 servings)

1	small head Boston lettuce	1
1	small leaf lettuce	1
2	Belgian endives, cored	2
1	small radiccio lettuce, cored	1
1	garlic clove, peeled and halved	1
3 tbsp	olive oil	45 mL
2 tbsp	lemon juice	30 mL
1 tsp	Dijon mustard	5 mL
1 tbsp	chopped fresh parsley	15 mL
	salt and freshly ground pepper	

1 Wash all lettuce in plenty of cold water and dry thoroughly.

2 Rub sides of wooden salad bowl with cut side of garlic. Tear lettuce leaves into small pieces and place in bowl. Season with salt and pepper.

3 Place oil, lemon juice and mustard in small bowl. Season well and add parsley. Whisk together and pour over salad. Toss, correct seasoning and serve.

Cooking Mushrooms for Salads

1 lb	fresh mushrooms, cleaned	450 g
½ cup	dry white wine	125 mL
1 tsp	olive oil	5 mL
1	bay leaf	1
	salt and pepper	
	lemon juice	

1 Place mushrooms and remaining ingredients in saucepan. Pour in cold water to cover mushrooms by three quarters. Cover with waxed paper touching surface of mushrooms and bring to boil.

2 Reduce heat to low and cook mushrooms 6 to 8 minutes.

3 Remove pan from heat and let mushrooms cool in liquid. Drain well before using.

4 If desired, mushrooms can be stored for later use. Keep in cooking liquid, cover tightly and refrigerate.

Cooked Salad Dressing
(4 to 6 servings)

1 tsp	sugar	5 mL
2 tbsp	flour	30 mL
2 tbsp	water	30 mL
2 tsp	English mustard	10 mL
¼ cup	white vinegar	50 mL
½ cup	water	125 mL
2	eggs, beaten	2
1 tbsp	soft butter	15 mL
	salt and pepper	
	few drops of Tabasco sauce	
	cold milk	

1 Place sugar, flour, salt and pepper in bowl. Add 2 tbsp (30 mL) water and mix together with whisk. Add mustard, vinegar and ½ cup (125 mL) water; incorporate with whisk.

2 Transfer mixture to saucepan and cook 3 minutes over low heat. Stir constantly during cooking. Remove pan from heat.

3 Incorporate eggs and butter, whisking until smooth.

4 Pour mixture into top part of double boiler. Cook 2 minutes over low heat, mixing constantly. Season with Tabasco sauce.

5 Transfer dressing to bowl and let cool. Thin with cold milk to reach desired consistency. Serve over lettuce and vegetable salads.

Homemade Mayonnaise
(8 to 10 servings)

2	egg yolks	2
1 tbsp	Dijon mustard	15 mL
1 ¼ cups	olive oil	300 mL
1 tbsp	lemon juice or white vinegar	15 mL
	salt and pepper	

1 Place egg yolks in bowl. Add salt, pepper and mustard. Whisk together for 1 minute.

2 When egg yolks thicken, begin adding oil drop by drop. It is important to whisk constantly. As mixture thickens, increase flow of oil to thin stream. Taste mayonnaise and add more oil if desired.

3 Whisk in lemon juice or vinegar. Correct seasoning.

4 To store mayonnaise, stir in 1 tbsp (15 mL) of hot water. Cover with plastic wrap touching surface and refrigerate for up to 3 days.

Mustard Vinaigrette
(6 to 8 servings)

I	egg yolk	I
I tbsp	Dijon mustard	15 mL
I	shallot, peeled and chopped	I
¼ cup	balsamic vinegar	50 mL
I cup	olive oil	250 mL
I tbsp	chopped fresh parsley	15 mL
	salt and pepper	
	few drops of lemon juice	
	cayenne pepper to taste	

1 Place egg yolk and mustard in bowl. Add shallot and vinegar; season well.

2 Incorporate oil in thin stream, whisking constantly. Add few drops of lemon juice and cayenne pepper to taste. Add parsley.

This vinaigrette keeps well in glass jar with tight-fitting lid. Refrigerate for up to 3 days.

Mayonnaise with Fresh Tomato
(6 to 8 servings)

1 tsp	olive oil	5 mL
2	medium tomatoes, cored and diced	2
1	garlic clove, peeled, crushed and chopped	1
1	shallot, peeled and chopped	1
1 tsp	tarragon	5 mL
1 ½ cups	Homemade Mayonnaise (see p. 85)	375 mL
	salt and pepper	
	pinch of crushed chilies	

1 Heat oil in sauté pan over medium heat. Add tomatoes, garlic, shallot and all seasonings. Cook 12 minutes over medium heat.

2 Pass mixture through food mill or blender. Place purée in bowl and set aside to cool.

3 Add ¼ cup (50 mL) or more of tomato mixture to Homemade Mayonnaise. Correct seasoning and serve with a variety of salads.

Tapenade
(4 to 6 servings)

I cup	pitted black olives	250 mL
4	anchovy fillets, drained and chopped	4
3 tbsp	lemon juice	45 mL
¾ cup	olive oil	175 mL
	salt and pepper	

1 Place olives and anchovies in food processor; purée. Transfer mixture to bowl and stir in lemon juice.

2 Add oil and whisk to incorporate. Season well with salt and pepper.

Use tapenade as a condiment for fresh vegetables, cold meats and fish.

Light Chili Mayonnaise
(4 to 6 servings)

½ cup	mayonnaise	125 mL
2 tbsp	buttermilk	30 mL
2	blanched garlic cloves, puréed	2
I tbsp	chili sauce	15 mL
	salt and pepper	
	lemon juice to taste	

1 Mix all ingredients together in small bowl. Correct seasoning and serve.

Basic Vinaigrette
(4 to 6 servings)

2 tbsp	white or red wine vinegar	30 mL
6 tbsp	olive oil	90 mL
1 tsp	chopped fresh parsley (optional)	5 mL
1 tsp	chopped fresh tarragon (optional)	5 mL
1 tsp	chopped fresh chives (optional)	5 mL
	salt and freshly ground pepper	

1 Place vinegar in bowl. Add salt and pepper.

2 Add oil and whisk to incorporate. Add herbs if using and mix well.

3 Correct seasoning and serve.

Use this vinaigrette over green salads.

Tomato Vinaigrette
(6 to 8 servings)

2	garlic cloves, peeled and sliced	2
3 tbsp	lemon juice	45 mL
3 tbsp	wine vinegar	45 mL
1/2 cup	olive oil	125 mL
1/2 tsp	sugar	2 mL
2 tbsp	tomato sauce	30 mL
1/4 tsp	English mustard	1 mL
1 tbsp	chopped fresh parsley	15 mL
	pepper	

1 In mixing bowl, combine all ingredients. Cover and marinate 1 hour in refrigerator.

2 Remove garlic before using. Serve over vegetable salads.

Soy Sauce Salad Dressing
(4 to 6 servings)

1/2 cup	cottage cheese	125 mL
4 tbsp	sour cream	60 mL
1/2 cup	buttermilk	125 mL
1 tbsp	Dijon mustard	15 mL
1 tsp	wine vinegar	5 mL
1/2 tsp	soy sauce	2 mL
	salt and pepper	
	few drops of Tabasco sauce	
	few drops of Worcestershire sauce	

1 Place all ingredients in food processor. Blend together and correct seasoning.

2 Refrigerate for up to 3 days, covered, until ready to use.

Cottage Cheese Blender Dressing

(4 to 6 servings)

1 cup	cottage cheese	250 mL
½ cup	mayonnaise	125 mL
¼ cup	plain yogurt	50 mL
2	blanched garlic cloves, puréed	2
1 tsp	Dijon mustard	5 mL
1 tbsp	white vinegar	15 mL
	pinch of sugar	
	few drops of lemon juice	
	few drops of Tabasco sauce	
	salt and pepper	

1 Place cottage cheese in food processor and purée. Add remaining ingredients and blend until incorporated.

2 Correct seasoning and serve with vegetable salads.

Sauce Rémoulade
(serves 6 to 8)

1 ½ cups	Homemade Mayonnaise (see p. 85)	375 mL
2 tbsp	Dijon mustard	30 mL
2 tbsp	capers	30 mL
1	large pickle, finely chopped	1
1 tbsp	chopped fresh parsley	15 mL
1 tbsp	chopped fresh tarragon	15 mL
2	anchovy fillets, drained and chopped	2
¼	yellow bell pepper, steamed, skinned and chopped	¼
	few drops of Tabasco sauce	
	freshly ground pepper	

1 Place all ingredients in bowl. Mix together until well blended. Correct seasoning and chill before serving.

A classic French sauce, rémoulade accompanies cold meats, fish, shellfish and egg dishes.

Tartar Sauce
(6 to 8 servings)

1 ½ cups	Homemade Mayonnaise (see p. 85)	375 mL
2	hard-boiled eggs, diced	2
1 tbsp	capers	15 mL
1	pickle, finely chopped	1
1 tsp	chopped fresh parsley	5 mL
1 tsp	chopped fresh chives	5 mL
1	shallot, peeled and chopped	1
	salt and pepper	
	cayenne pepper to taste	
	lemon juice to taste	

1 Mix all ingredients together until well blended.

Serve with cold or hot fish salads.

Thick Egg Vinaigrette
(4 to 6 servings)

1 tbsp	Dijon mustard	15 mL
1	egg yolk	1
2 tbsp	wine vinegar	30 mL
6 tbsp	olive oil	90 mL
2	blanched garlic cloves, puréed	2
2 tbsp	sour cream	30 mL
	salt and pepper	
	lemon juice to taste	

1 Place mustard, egg yolk, salt and pepper in small bowl. Whisk together. Add vinegar and mix again.

2 Pour in oil and whisk until vinaigrette becomes thick. Mix in garlic and sour cream. Season well.

3 Add lemon juice to taste and serve.

Blue Cheese Dressing
(4 to 6 servings)

⅓ cup	plain yogurt	75 mL
⅓ cup	cottage cheese	75 mL
½ cup	light mayonnaise	125 mL
½ cup	crumbled blue cheese	125 mL
	few drops of Worcestershire sauce	
	few drops of lemon juice	
	salt and freshly ground pepper	
	pinch of paprika	

1 Mix all ingredients, except blue cheese, together until smooth.

2 Season well and add blue cheese. Mix and serve over lettuce.

Light Mayonnaise for Vegetable Salads
(4 to 6 servings)

⅓ cup	mayonnaise	75 mL
1 tbsp	sour cream	15 mL
1 tsp	Dijon mustard	5 mL
1 tbsp	chopped fresh chives	15 mL
	salt and pepper	
	cayenne pepper to taste	
	juice of ½ lemon	

1 Mix all ingredients together in small bowl. Correct seasoning and serve.

Ranch Dressing
(4 to 6 servings)

2	garlic cloves, blanched	2
1 cup	buttermilk	250 mL
¾ cup	mayonnaise	175 mL
½ tsp	celery seeds	2 mL
1 tsp	dill	5 mL
½ tsp	English mustard	2 mL
	lemon juice to taste	
	salt and pepper	
	pinch of paprika	

1 To blanch garlic cloves, cook in boiling water for about 4 minutes. Remove cloves from water and let cool; peel and purée.

2 Place all ingredients in food processor; blend until smooth. Correct seasoning and serve.

Index